The GARDEN LOVERS

BOOK OF DAYS

EXLEY

 NOTES

NOTES

*It is wonderful how much work one can find to
do in so tiny a plot of ground. But in the latter
weeks of June there comes a time when I can
begin to take breath and rest a little from these
difficult yet pleasant labors; an interval when I
may take time to consider, a morning when I
may seek the hammock in the shady piazza,
and, looking across my happy flower beds, let
the sweet day sink deep into my heart.*

CELIA THAXTER

NOTES

_____

_____

_____

_____

_____

_____

_____

_____

_____

_____

_____

_____

_____

_____

_____

_____

_____

_____

_____

_____

There's not a pair of legs so thin,
there's not a head so thick,
There's not a hand so weak and white,
not yet a heart so sick,
But it can find some needful work that's
crying to be done,
For the Glory of the Garden glorifieth everyone.

RUDYARD KIPLING

JANUARY

1

2

3

4

5

6

7

In green old gardens, hidden away
From sight of revel and sound of strife...
Here may I live what life I please
Married and buried out of sight.

VIOLET FARRE

JANUARY

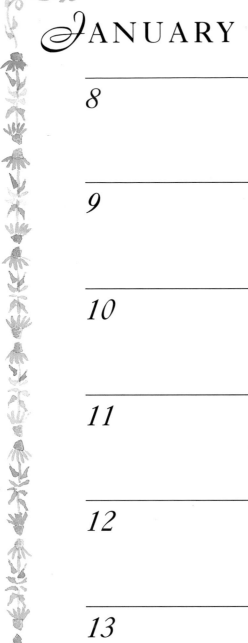

8

9

10

11

12

13

14

THE SPRING
JACOB GRIMMER
Bridgeman Art Library:
Lille, Musée des
Beaux-Arts

To own a bit of ground, to scratch it with a hoe,
to plant seeds and watch the renewal of life -
this is the commonest delight of the race, the most
satisfactory thing a man can do.

CHARLES DUDLEY WARNER

$\mathcal{J}$ANUARY

15

16

17

18

19

20

21

Nature to be commanded, must be obeyed. FRANCIS BACON

JANUARY

22

23

24

25

26

27

28

HOTHOUSE
FLOWERS
*PIERRE
AUGUSTE
RENOIR*
Bridgeman Art Library:
Hamburg, Kunsthalle

How often I regret that plants cannot talk. VITA SACKVILLE-WEST

JANUARY/FEBRUARY

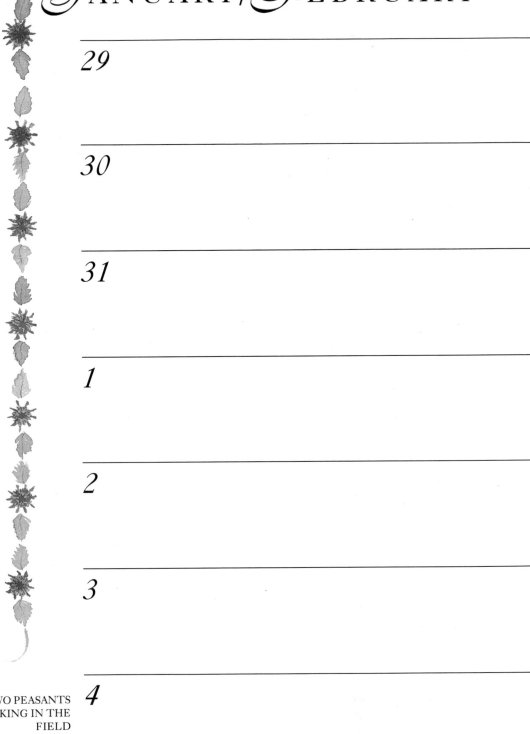

29

30

31

1

2

3

4

Shed no tear! O shed no tear!
The flower will bloom another year.
Weep no more! Weep no more!
Young buds sleep in the root's white core.

JOHN KEATS

FEBRUARY

5

6

7

8

9

10

11

EARLY SPRING
IN A SUMMER
VILLAGE
*Edward
Wilkins Waite*
Bridgeman Art Library

So deeply is the gardener's instinct implanted in my soul, I really love the tools with which I work, - the iron fork, the spade, the hoe, the rake, the trowel, and the watering-pot are pleasant objects in my eyes.

CELIA THAXTER

$\mathcal{F}$EBRUARY

12

13

14

15

16

17

18

BONJOUR
MONSIEUR
GAUGUIN

PAUL GAUGUIN
Bridgeman Art Library:
London, Christie & Co.

Happiness is a bare black stump showing a speck of green. PAM BROWN

$\mathcal{F}$EBRUARY

19

20

21

22

23

24

25

THE KITCHEN
GARDEN
B.J. DE HOOG
Bridgeman Art Library:
Hamm-Rhynern, Josef
Mensing Gallery

A gardener knows all that needs to be done.
And why. And yet is still astounded by the miracle.

PAM BROWN

FEBRUARY/MARCH

26

27

28/29

1

2

3

4

PEACH TREES IN BLOSSOM
VINCENT VAN GOGH
Bridgeman Art Library: London, Courtauld Institute Galleries

To sow seeds and plant out, to graft and propagate, whether it be peas and beans, apples and plums, roses and peonies, is to make one's own positive stake in that future, a gesture, declaring that there will be weeks, months, years ahead. And he who plants sapling trees, which will not arrive at their full maturity for fifty or a hundred years, is not only an optimist but a benefactor to coming generations.

SUSAN HILL

MARCH

5

6

7

8

9

10

11

PLUM TREES IN BLOSSOM
CAMILLE PISSARRO
Bridgeman Art Library: Private Collection

*What was Paradise? but a Garden, an
Orchard of Trees and Herbs, full of pleasure,
and nothing there but delights...What can your
eye desire to see, your nose to smell, your mouth
to take that is not to be had in an Orchard?*

WILLIAM LAWSON

MARCH

12

13

14

15

16

17

18

APPLE BLOSSOM
Albert Ernst Muhlig
Fine Art Photographic Library

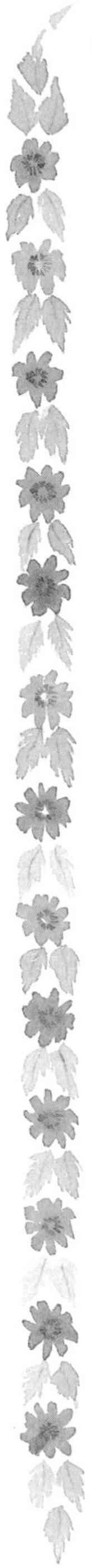

*Little strips in front of roadside cottages have a
simple and tender charm that one may look for in vain in
gardens of greater pretension. And the old garden flowers
seem to know that there they are seen at their best; for where
else can one see such wall-flowers, or double daisies, or
white rose bushes; such clustering masses of perennial
peas, or such well-kept flowery edgings of
pink, or thrift, or London pride?*

GERTRUDE JEKYLL

MARCH

19

20

21

22

23

24

25

AN OLD MANOR
HOUSE AND
GARDEN
T. TYNDALE
Bridgeman Art Library:
London, Christopher
Wood Gallery

All gardeners know better than other gardeners. CHINESE PROVERB

MARCH/APRIL

26

27

28

29

30

31

1

A SUMMER
GARDEN WITH
MADONNA LILIES
L. STANNARD
*Bridgeman Art Library:
London, Christopher
Wood Gallery*

APRIL

2

3

4

5

6

7

8

THE VEGETABLE GARDEN WITH TREES IN BLOSSOM, PONTOISE IN SPRING

C. PISSARRO

Bridgeman Art Library: Paris, Musée d'Orsay

Our garden is now a wilderness of sweets. The violets, sweet briar, and primroses perfume the air, and the thrushes are full of melody and make our concert complete. It is the pleasantest music I have heard this year, and refreshes my spirits without the alloy of a tumultuous crowd, which attends all the other concerts.

MRS. DELANY

$\mathcal{A}$PRIL

9

10

11

12

13

14

15

NEAR EXETER
*HAROLD
SUTTON
PALMER*
*Fine Art
Photographic Library*

*. . . But there was something better than
a planned beauty in the place; generations
of men had made a hard-won living from it
and their women, working as hard or harder,
had found time to sow a few seeds, to put a
flower root in the ground and keep the beds
clear of weeds. The beauty had come, as it were,
from rare moments of leisure, it had survived
and increased and was all the greater for its
subordination to homelier necessities.*

E. H. YOUNG

APRIL

16

17

18

19

20

21

22

*I have seen him out there among his flowers,
petting them, talking to them, coaxing them till
they simply had to grow.*

J. M. BARRIE

$\mathcal{A}$PRIL

23

24

25

26

27

28

29

KINGS MANOR
GARDEN AT EAST
HENDRED
C. FLOWER
Bridgeman Art Library:
London, Christopher
Wood Gallery

April in New England is like first love. GLADYS TABER

APRIL / MAY

30

1

2

3

4

5

6

God the first garden made, and the first city Cain. ABRAHAM COWLEY

MAY

7

8

9

10

11

12

13

CUTTING HEDGES
CAMILLE
PISSARRO
Scala: Florence, Galleria
d'Arte Moderna

The pleasure that there is in
the actual, practical work of a garden,
must be tried before it can be understood.
Liking for it will grow by exercise,
even when not felt naturally; for
of this healthy enjoyment may be said,
what is generally remarked of more
doubtful pleasures, that "it only
needs a beginning".

HENRIETTA WILSON, 1864

MAY

14

15

16

17

18

19

20

A WALLED
GARDEN WITH
STATUES
A. COX
Bridgeman Art Library:
London, Christopher
Wood Gallery

Man was lost and saved in a garden. BLAISE PASCAL

MAY

21

22

23

24

25

26

27

POND IN THE GARDEN OF RAKU-RAKU-TEI, HIKONE

A. PARSONS

Bridgeman Art Library: London, Chris Beetles Ltd.

28

29

30

31

1

2

3

But though an old man, I am but a young gardener. THOMAS JEFFERSON

JUNE

4

5

6

7

8

9

10

As is the garden such is the gardener.   HEBREW PROVERB

JUNE

11

12

13

14

15

16

17

THE GARDEN
PATH
*JAMES
MATTHEWS*
*Fine Art Photographic
Library: Chester,
City Wall Gallery*

Nothing is more the child of art than a garden. SIR WALTER SCOTT

JAMES MATTHEWS.

JUNE

18

19

20

21

22

23

24

*She <u>knew</u>. She knew flowers not only by their
names - English and Latin - not only by their
families, nor their structures, nor their habits -
she knew them in their essence. It is
extraordinarily difficult to explain what I
mean, but if you had seen her bend over a
winter iris, you would realize what I meant. . . .
There was a magic in her touch. At any rate,
the iris over which she had bent was
the only iris which bloomed that winter.*

BEVERLEY NICHOLS

25

26

27

28

29

30

1

YOUNG GIRL IN
THE GARDEN AT
MONTMARTRE
RENOIR
Bridgeman Art Library:
London, Christie & Co.

Loveliest of all, carnations and pinks,
Smelling of heady clove, sharp nutmeg,
Lining the borders of the smooth lawn,
With mignonette, fragrant verbena.
I make a posy of them all in my mind,
Remember their colours and shapes, when
The garden has only the flowers of the frost,
The smell of dead bonfires.

LEONARD CLARK

JULY

2

3

4

5

6

7

8

AN ENGLISH
GARDEN
P. R. CRAFT
Bridgeman Art Library:
York, City Art Gallery

A garden makes sure you always have something to worry about. PAM BROWN

JULY

9

10

11

12

13

14

15

Hast thou loved the wood-rose and left it on its stalk? RALPH WALDO EMERSON

JULY

16

17

18

19

20

21

22

IN THE GARDEN,
1885

*CHARLES
ANGRAND*
Bridgeman Art Library:
Rouen, Musée des
Beaux-Arts

. . . a real gardener is not a man who
cultivates flowers; he is a man who
cultivates the soil.

KAREL CAPETE

JULY

23

24

25

26

27

28

29

Is not a nosegay plucked from one's own beds and borders more valued than twenty times the quantity would be derived from another source?

GLENNY'S HANDBOOK OF PRACTICAL GARDENING, c. 1855

JULY/AUGUST

30

31

1

2

3

4

CRIMSON RAMBLER AT CLANDON PARK

Thomas Hunn

Bridgeman Art Library: London, Christopher Wood Gallery

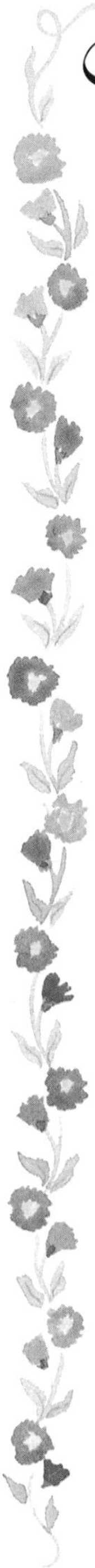

5

*It would never occur to most gardeners to write
a poem or paint a picture. Most gardens are
the only artistic effort their owners ever make.*

HUGH JOHNSON

AUGUST

6

7

8

9

10

11

12

SPRING
AFTERNOON
*JACQUES
JOSEPH TISSOT*
*Fine Art Photographic
Library*

$\mathscr{A}$UGUST

13

14

15

16

17

18

19

AN ITALIAN
BALCONY
*ERNEST
ARTHUR ROWE*
*Bridgeman Art Library:
London, Chris Beetles Ltd.*

There is no such thing as an
ordinary flower.

CHARLOTTE GRAY

AUGUST

20

21

22

23

24

25

26

To get the best results you must talk to your vegetables. PRINCE CHARLES

27

28

29

30

31

1

2

THE ARTIST'S
GARDEN
ARTHUR LEGGE
Bridgeman Art Library:
Warwickshire,
Fine-Lines (Fine Art)

A garden without trees scarcely deserves to be called a garden. CANON H. ELLACOMBE

SEPTEMBER

3

4

5

6

7

8

9

TWO WOMEN
WALKING IN A
PARK (DETAIL)
*VINCENT VAN
GOGH*
Scala: Leningrad,
Hermitage Museum

If you truly love Nature, you will find beauty everywhere. VINCENT VAN GOGH

SEPTEMBER

10

11

12

13

14

15

16

THE APPLE
GATHERERS
FREDERICK
MORGAN
Bridgeman Art Library:
London, Roy Miles
Fine Paintings

A garden is not for giving or taking.
A garden is for all.

FRANCIS HODGSON BURNETT

SEPTEMBER

17

18

19

20

21

22

23

*A modest garden contains, for those that
know how to look and to wait,
more instruction than a library.*

HENRI FREDERIC AMIEL

SEPTEMBER

24

25

26

27

28

29

30

THE ORANGE GATHERERS
JOHN WILLIAM WATERHOUSE
Bridgeman Art Library: London, Christie & Co.

OCTOBER

1

2

3

4

5

6

THE TANGLE OF AUTUMN, TEMPLE GRAFTON, WARWICKSHIRE
G. H. HUGHES
Bridgeman Art Library: Christopher Wood Gallery

7

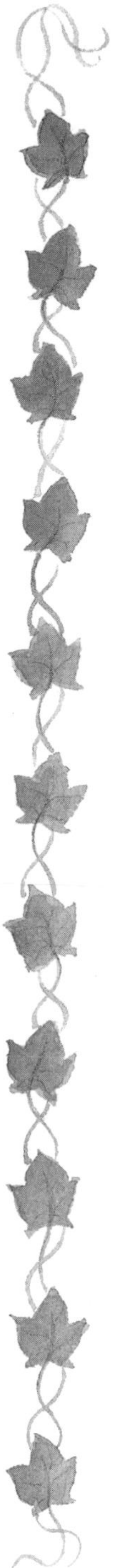

The best gardens are something of a muddle.
They have an air of happy accident, they look a
little careless, however carefully in fact the whole
has been planned. Things have grown up and
flourished cheek by jowl, like a large family of children,
some natural, some adopted, some short and some tall,
some further advanced for their age than others ...
and they tumble about together then fall into each
other's arms, or else squabble perpetually until
they are separated, in just such a way.

SUSAN HILL

OCTOBER

8

9

10

11

12

13

14

THE CHERRY PICKER
BERTHE MORISOT
Bridgeman Art Library: Paris, Private Collection

OCTOBER

15

16

17

18

19

20

21

GENTLEMAN READING IN A GARDEN
KARL SPITZWEG
Bridgeman Art Library: Stockholm, National Museum

*It is good to be alone in a garden at dawn or dark so
that all its shy presences may haunt you and possess you
in a reverie of suspended thought.*

JAMES DOUGLAS

OCTOBER

22

23

24

25

26

27

28

A FLEMISH
GARDEN
*HENRI DE
BRAEKELEER*
*Bridgeman Art Library:
London, Victoria and
Albert Museum*

I love my garden! dearly love
That little spot of ground!
There's not, me thinks, (though I may err
In partial pride) a pleasanter
In all the country round.

HENRIETTA WILSON

OCTOBER/NOVEMBER

29

30

31

1

2

3

4

A CORNER OF
LOUVECIENNES,
C. 1870

*CAMILLE
PISSARRO*
Bridgeman Art Library:
London, Christie & Co.

A man does not plant a tree for himself; he plants it for posterity. A. SMITH

NOVEMBER

5

6

7

8

9

10

11

He who plants a garden plants happiness. CHINESE PROVERB

NOVEMBER

12

13

14

15

16

17

18

The garden that is finished is dead. H. E. BATES

November

19

20

21

22

23

24

25

In order to live off a garden, you practically have to live in it. F. MCKINNEY HUBBARD

26

27

28

29

30

1

2

THE VIRGINIA
CREEPER
WILLIAM
LUNDSAY
WINDUS
Bridgeman Art Library:
Roy Miles Fine Paintings

One of the greatest gifts of a perfect garden is the gift of solitude, and that is generally beyond the power of the little cottage plot to offer; but, as a source of infinite pleasure to its owner, as a source of pleasure to all who pass by, as a cheering feature . . . and as a great force tending towards contentment and peace, the cottage garden is beyond all praise."

HARRY ROBERTS

DECEMBER

3

4

5

6

7

8

9

FRIARS WORKING
IN THEIR
KITCHEN GARDEN
G. STARNINA
Scala: Florence,
Uffizi Gallery

DECEMBER

10

11

12

13

14

15

16

<u>THE ANCIENT GAMES OF FLOWERS</u>

In the cottage of the rudest peasant,
In ancestral homes, whose crumbling towers,
Speaking of the Past unto the Present,
Tell us of the ancient Games of Flowers;

In all places then, and in all seasons,
Flowers expand their light and soul-like wings,
Teaching us, by most persuasive reasons,
How akin they are to human beings.

POETRY OF FLOWERS, 1890

December

17

18

19

20

21

22

23

*Lastly, love your flowers. By some subtle
sense the dear things always detect their
friends, and for them they will live longer
and bloom more freely than they ever
will for a stranger.*

JULIA S. BERRALL

DECEMBER

24

25

26

27

28

29

30

*For the last forty years of my life I have broken my
back, my fingernails, and sometimes my heart . . .*

VITA SACKVILLE-WEST

DECEMBER/JANUARY

31

1

2

3

4

5

6